Keith Ha...

Dorking
and District
IN OLD PHOTOGRAPHS

David Knight

Walter J. Rose (1857–1954).

Introduction

This story begins in 1857. Queen Victoria had been on the throne for twenty years, the Great Exhibition in Hyde Park had been and gone, a Peace Treaty had been signed in Paris ending the Crimean War and Walter Rose was born. Now the birth of a baby son to an agricultural labourer in a small Surrey village was not destined to make much of an impression upon the record books, but possibly his real worth has remained hidden until now.

John and Jane Rose raised the young Walter and his siblings, Ernest and Amos, in Westcott, sending them to the village school where Walter was to see the headmaster, Charles Brown, experimenting with the new art-form of photography. The wet-collodion process, where the user had to coat his glass plates with light-sensitive 'emulsion' before use, was still firmly established and was not to be ousted until the 1870s, with the introduction of gelatin dry plates.

Walter was not able to follow a career in photography upon leaving school, for it was chiefly a fashionable pastime for the leisured and wealthy class, so he entered service at Holcombe on Westcott Common as a gardener alongside his brother Ernest. He attempted to break free and applied for a post in the library at Harrow School upon the advice of the art teacher, William Egerton Hine, a Westcott resident and friend of the Roses. But to no avail. A career in photography beckoned, and shortly he was to marry Ellen. They went to live at 1 Westcott Street, converted the garden shed into a dark-room and erected a wooden studio in the front garden.

The principal source of income would have derived from family portraiture, commissions from wealthy landowners and the printing of picture postcards, which were sweeping the nation by the early twentieth century as a collecting craze, sustaining many a small-time village photographer.

Walter and Ellen had no children, but raised their niece Dolly, whose mother had died on the day that she was born. Walter clearly doted on this young girl and took her photograph on many occasions. As she grew older, Dolly was able to help Walter process his plates and to make prints from them, and sometimes she even turned the camera on Walter. The business struggled along into the 1920s, by which time Walter had reached retiring age, and thereafter he only took the occasional photograph.

Ellen Rose died in 1935 and Dolly remained to look after Walter, who lived to be 97. During his years of inactivity the precious glass plates were stored in the shed where they came to little harm.

During the 1960s David Knight was busy compiling his own archive of Westcott's history and, as he was a friend of the Roses, Dolly passed on to him her uncle's invaluable pictorial record of the area in the form of 900 glass negatives, lantern slides and photographic prints. Lately David has allowed me complete access to this 'treasure trove' and I feel proud to be able to print, in many cases for the first time in ninety years, from Walter Rose's splendid plates.

So, thank you to Dolly for having kept this horde of plates safe, thank you to David for recognizing their worth, but chiefly thank you to Walter Rose for opening up to us a small window on his world.

Wearing a typical smock of the period, this farmer fits beautifully Gertrude Jekyll's description of the garb. 'The old carter's smock-frock, or round frock, still lingering, but on its way to becoming extinct, is centuries old. No better thing has ever been devised for any kind of outdoor wear that admits of the use of an outer garment. It turns an astonishing amount of wet, especially when of the ordinary local pattern that has a wide turn-over collar, something like a sailor's, but coming square over the shoulders in front and behind. The frock is cut square; of two whole widths of the stuff, with side seams only. The shaping is made by the close gathering, either over the whole back and front, or in two panels on the breast and back near the buttons. It can be worn either way about; back and front are alike. It sits just as well either way. The sleeves are put in very low: not on the shoulder, but some inches down the arm. There is a worked gathering at their insertion, and also at the wristband, to bring the greater width of the sleeve into the size of the wrist. The material is a strong, tough, closely-woven linen. It was in four colourings: light and dark grey, olive green and white.'

The harshness of a cottager's life shows in the appearance of these two Westcott men. On the left stands John Rose, father of Walter, an agricultural labourer, while on the right is a young man whom Dolly Rose only recalled ever being called 'that boy-chap'.

Walter Rose's studio. Ellen Rose plants the clematis that is seen in another photograph (p. 10) climbing over the trellis fence. The glass panes in the roof of the studio allowed shadow-free north light to illuminate the model within.

Walter Rose's garden shed was adapted to suit his use as a darkroom while also serving his wife Ellen, seen here, as a laundry. His collection of 900 glass-plate negatives was stored in this wooden building after his death in 1957, and was passed on to David Knight by Dolly Rose in 1962. After Dolly's death in 1991 the darkroom was demolished by the landlord to make way for a new kitchen and bathroom.

The rear view of Walter Rose's humble cottage, 1 Westcott Street, with his wife Ellen sitting in front of a splendid clematis clambering over rustic fencing. 'It is a sign of careful gardening and good upbringing, when little boys of a family are seen on the roads with old shovels and little improvised hand carts, collecting horse droppings. It means that the plants will have a nourishing surface mulching that will be much to their benefit.' (Gertrude Jekyll, *Old West Surrey*.)

Walter and Ellen Rose's wedding, 1897. Forty-year-old Walter married Ellen in 1897, and this group of guests includes his sister Alice, mother of Dolly, who is seen here holding the infant Nell.

'Dolly's first tea party', 1 July 1908. Outside the back door of 1 Westcott Street, Ellen Rose has laid out a birthday tea for the 1-year-old Dolly. Her sister Nell sits next to her, with young playmates completing this charming group photograph.

Dolly, September 1908. One-year-old Dolly rides in her toy cart, probably home-made, clutching a toy monkey.

Dolly sleeping in a splendid perambulator, which carried its occupant in a seated, not lying, position.

The Rose family displays the children's toys, probably nothing special in their day but highly prized by today's collectors.

With her toys around as usual, Dolly entertains a friend to tea, 1910. They have fairy cakes and their own small tea set on an improvised table.

Dolly, wearing a bonnet, plays hostess to eight playmates in the garden at 1 Westcott Street.

JULY 4 '10

Dolly's third birthday. The splendid perambulator in which she was wheeled as a baby now serves as a perfect, albeit rather large, carriage for her toys.

One year on, and we can see that more toys have arrived at 1 Westcott Street. China dolls vie for position with a teddy bear, a toy rabbit and several wheel-along toys.

Alice Rose died very shortly after giving birth to Dolly, her third child, and Dolly is seen here tending her mother's grave at Westcott church. The headstone was made by W.M. Woodland of West Street, Dorking, in 1908, and cost £4 10s. 0d. A fee of 13s. 6d. was paid to the vicar and clerk for the funeral.

OCT. 13. 12

Dolly taking the cats for a ride in the pushchair, 1912.

Dolly Rose, 1913.

Dolly, 1914. As she grew older, Dolly shifted her affections from toys to the family pets. Here a kitten is chosen as her partner for a photograph.

During the First World War the Rose family found times hard, as did most. Ellen Rose took on the role of postwoman during a period when the regular staff were at war or redeployed.

Nell Rose, Walter Rose's niece and sister of Dolly. She lived with her father Amos in Milton Street and worked for many years as a seamstress and general maid at Bury Hill in Logmore Lane. Nell remained a spinster and in her later years moved into the Westcott Street home of her sister Dolly, where she remained until her death in 1987.

Walter Rose's nephew, Ernest, photographed in the studio during the First World War. He is wearing standard issue winter wear for a gunner in the Royal Artillery.

5

Wedding group, Westcott. The ladies are sporting some fine hats, and a feather boa adorns the lady on the far left of the back row. Photographic materials were not very sensitive, requiring rather long shutter speeds, which very often resulted in slightly blurred images – particularly among fidgety children.

The Johnson family, Westcott. This well-known local family came to the village store in the 1880s, taking over a business that had been established in the 1830s. John Johnson was the first boy to be christened at Westcott church in 1852 and was later to become the first landlord of the Bricklayer's Arms, in 1899. The village store and post office advertised itself as a family grocer and baker, also selling paraffin, benzolene, china, earthenware, boots and shoes. The Johnson family continued to run the business until the 1960s.

Charles Collins RBA, RCA and family. The artist was photographed at his home in Dorking, possibly in Horsham Road. The children all appear well dressed, which suggests that Collins earned a good living as a painter.

Three generations of the Balchin family stand outside their Chapel Lane, Westcott, home in which they all lived at one time. The upturned flower pots atop the dahlia stakes indicate that a gardener in the family was using a favourite method of trapping earwigs, which damaged the plants.

The Steadman family, 1917. David Knight's mother's family was photographed by
Walter in the studio at Westcott Street, having walked the short distance from Chapel
Lane. Emily Steadman is with her children Ethel, Florence and William.

This working-class wedding group is posing outside the Graces' house in Heath Rise, Westcott. The bride, groom and bride's mother are seated. An Indian campaign veteran can be seen, and there is also a guest clutching a tambourine, possibly looking forward to entertaining the other guests at the reception.

The Razell family, seated in front of their cottage in Milton Street, 1896. William started work aged 9 for the Barclays at Bury Hill House. With his wife, Alice, he raised eight children on a wage of 18s. per week.

Westcott School, *c*. 1900. The original Victorian building, which housed the infant and junior classes, was added to in 1912 to provide two further classrooms and a hall, extending the scope of the education provided. These additions were provided at the expense of a schoolmaster's house, which was promised but never built.

School group, *c.* 1914. Some of the children are dressed in sailor suits, while other girls wear what appear to be Girl Guide style uniforms. The front row reveals a diversity of footwear from hob-nail boots to calf length lace-up boots.

Not only was the pinafore an attractive form of dress, but it was also eminently suitable for keeping the cotton frock clean during practical lessons such as cookery, where the ingredients for making pancakes could so easily end up in a place other than that intended.

Westcott School headmaster, Mr Johnson, taking an art class, during which using the left hand was positively discouraged. This was certainly a Draconian measure by today's standards.

While the girls were being educated in matters domestic, the boys were busy tending the school garden, here showing a fine crop of cabbages and broad beans. Sticks are in place for runner beans to climb along. The headmaster, Mr Johnson, is seen supervising.

While the boys were at their gardening lesson, the girls were being educated in the art of washing and changing baby. With the help of dolls, these young children were taught the finer points of motherhood. Many of them were surely destined to become nannies or nursemaids, while others were probably having to care for younger siblings at home.

Many of the boys would be leaving school to enter service as gardeners or farm labourers, but even those who were to follow other careers would surely have been grateful for a sound knowledge of gardening to help them maintain a degree of self-sufficiency in adult life, where many mouths could be dependent upon a meagre wage. Here the subject being taught is that of grafting roses.

With the aid of a small coal-fired range, the girls in this cookery class are preparing the ingredients for either scones or a jam pudding. The recipe has not changed, but how long can it be since milk was measured in gills?

The boys were taught many garden skills as part of their curriculum, and here Mr Chalke of Milton Farm instructs the pupils in the art of bee-keeping, using hives placed in the school garden. Mr Johnson, the headmaster, looks on.

Miss 'Becky' Greathurst, an assistant teacher at Westcott School between 1879 and 1925, demonstrates the art of forming letters, while the junior pupils trace the characters with their forefingers in sand trays. As with the drawing class, no pupil can be seen using his or her left hand.

Sutton Abinger, *c.* 1905. Turning off the A25 at Abinger Hammer towards Holmbury St Mary takes one through this hamlet, which appears very much today as it did in this photograph.

Ellen Rose on her much used bicycle on the track outside Leylands, Wotton.

This is thought to be the first motor taxi in Westcott. Driven by Mr Shepherd, it is waiting outside the Wotton Hatch Hotel, having driven the Bartletts to their wedding reception.

Blackmore Turner opened his first butcher's shop at 61 South Street, Dorking, in 1892 and later moved to 50b High Street (now Seymours sports shop), at the same time opening a second branch at 31 Hampstead Road. In 1896 one of Turner's receipts puts the cost of a 9 lb 10 oz loin of beef at 6s. 10½d.

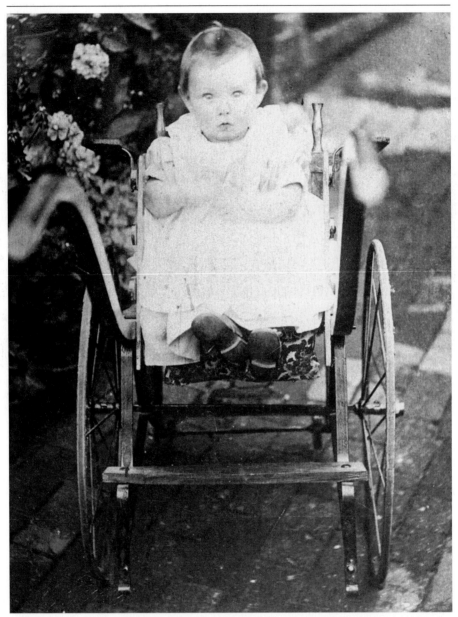

Wynn Smithers, 1892. Wynn's father was employed by the Barclays at Bury Hill House, and Wynn entered service herself at the age of 14, on an annual wage of £12. At the outbreak of the First World War she found herself doing essential work for the war effort, filling ammunition at the Woolwich Arsenal. She married Bill Wakefield in 1920 and bore him two sons. At the time of publication Mrs Smithers had just celebrated her 101st birthday in her home in Milton Street, and still ably bakes her own cakes and bread.

The Aldershot & District motor bus that plied for trade between Aldershot and Leatherhead in the 1920s. The driver and conductor still wear the jodhpurs and gaiters that were worn by their horse-driving predecessors, and this manner of dress continued for many years among professional drivers and chauffeurs.

This report was carried in the *Dorking Advertiser* on 4 July 1914: 'The dangerous corner in the main road at Westcott was the scene of a motor accident on Monday morning. Luckily the colliding vehicles were travelling at a very slow speed, or the consequences might have been serious. The motors concerned were a 'bus belonging to the Aldershot & District Traction Company, driven by William Rivers of Farnborough, and a private car belonging to Mr Fuchs of Roselawn, Westcott, driven by William Gale. At the time of the accident there were seven passengers in the 'bus, which was on its way to Guildford. The private car which was going towards Dorking was following another 'bus belonging to the Aldershot Company. When about to take the corner opposite Mr Smith's shop, the conductor signalled that he was stopping to pick up a passenger. Gale then passed the 'bus from behind on the offside and met the oncoming 'bus. Both collided and the impact wedged both together so effectually that it was some time before they could be separated. Mechanics were immediately despatched from Aldershot and they eventually cleared the obstruction. The damage to both vehicles was very considerable. A lady passenger in the 'bus was slightly hurt.'

Dorking Rural District Council steam roller, 1913. With the advent of tarmacked roads came the machinery necessary for its application. Dorking RDC housed its Aveling & Porter steam roller in the stables at Bury Hill from where it was driven to its destination for many years by Mr Laker, seen in the cab. The council sold this machine to Wards of Egham in the 1950s after forty years of service.

Horse-drawn tar boilers make ready for the first application of tarmacadam in
Westcott, 1904. 'Since motor traffic called for improved roads, many districts are
discontinuing the use of so much local material, and are using instead small angular
pieces of Norwegian granite. This has been proved in many districts to make the best
macadamised roads. The bands of ironstone previously referred to as being found in the
Folkestone Beds are also used locally for road mending, probably thus earning their
name of "car stone".' (Ellen Smith, *The Reigate Sheet.*)

Accident on Coast Hill, 1905. Five thousand bricks were strewn across the road when a traction engine from the Dorking Brick Company suffered mechanical failure with spectacular results. The engine drawing two trailers rolled backwards down the hill, forcing the trailers to jack-knife – one ending up on top of the other. The driver, Mr T.F. Tracey, was unhurt until he fell from one of the trailers while helping to clear the wreckage. He fell 'a distance of about seven feet, and his head striking the ground, he was rendered unconscious. Happily he quickly recovered, and was able to give his further assistance.'

Some relatives of the Roses visit Westcott in their impressive FN motor car.

Church Stile House, Cobham. A gentleman on a tricycle pauses alongside this magnificent house in Church Street, built in 1432.

Mr Ludlow. The splendidly attired coachman at Westcott House was in the employ of Mr Wills, who was related to the cigarette manufacturing family. Gertrude Jekyll recalled: 'I can remember when one could tell what a man was by his distinctive dress. How little of this remains; even the red caps of the brewers' vanmen are now but rarely seen.'

Milton Farm, Westcott, 1905. A fine pair of dappled grey shires are pulling a cart belonging to Kent & Chalke. Gertrude Jekyll writes of the carter's language, 'I have often wondered what may have been the origin of some of the curious words, or rather sounds, by which the carter communicates with his horses. "Woh" for "stop" is familiar to us all. For going forward the word of command is "pull up"; this is intelligible, though the words as uttered can hardly be recognized, but the alternatives "gee-whee" or "gee-whut-ah" or the still more mysterious "mither-wee" ("come to me" or "turn around") seem to be outside the bounds of either etymology or syntax.'

Morris Charman, carter.

Clearing up after a severe storm on 14 December 1907 was a much more strenuous affair than in 1987. Farm horses were hitched to the tree trunks that had been cut by hand, and of course the whole scene was observed by village folk.

Boxhill and Burford Bridge station, *c.* 1900. This magnificent building bears testimony to the importance of this station during the Victorian/Edwardian periods, when crowds would head south out of London on their high days and holidays to climb Box Hill. The station changed names many times – Westhumble until 1870, Boxhill and Burford Bridge until 1896, plain Boxhill until 1904, then Boxhill and Burford Bridge again. At the moment it is known as Boxhill and Westhumble.

Hole Hill Crossing, Westcott. The crossing-gate keeper's wife has closed the gates in preparation for an oncoming train heading for Reading.

Cycling became as popular among ladies as men in the early twentieth century, but the emancipation of women was still in its early days, and many lady bicyclists found that they were unable to find accommodation on country visits for some years to come.

Laying the main drains, Westcott, 1904. A group of forty-nine labourers, craftsmen and supervisors pose before the Surrey Trading Company's depot on Westcott Green. How many men would be required with today's machinery?

Drain laying, 1904. The main road (A25) was only about 12 ft wide where it passed along Sandrock Hill, Westcott, and there was certainly no need for traffic lights while the trench was being dug by spade and pick-axe for the laying of the main drains.

Frederick Molyneux, 1905. Mr Molyneux began service in the Post Office in 1870, retiring only on reaching the upper age limit of 60 years. For the duration of his thirty-five years' service he walked the Westcott round, an average of 20 miles every day, there being three deliveries daily. It was calculated that his 'long walk had covered a distance of 255,500 miles, or ten and a half times round the world'. On his retirement a fund was opened by Westcott post office and raised £17 1s. 6d. from a grateful village. Mr Molyneux wrote from his Rothes Road, Dorking, home: 'I beg to thank most sincerely all who have subscribed to the fund for the kind manner in which they have appreciated my services as a postman for a period of 35 years.'

Maintenance team, Bury Hill House. This team was responsible for the repair and upkeep of the fabric of this grand house, including plumbing, decorating, carpentry and building works. The role of the dog is not recorded.

Gardeners, Bury Hill House, *c.* 1900. A team of fifteen was required to tend the grounds of this large estate, which at this time included the Nower, given for public use by Lt.-Col. R.W. Barclay in 1931 amid much ceremony.

*yours truly
Alf Wilkins*

Alf Wilkins, chimney sweep. This photograph, taken in the studio, was used by Alf Wilkins as a Christmas card, sent out from his Falkland Hill, Dorking, home.

Schools gave children the occasional day off for certain rural activities that were vital to local farming communities. Picking potatoes was very labour intensive, hence the use of schoolchildren, who were able to earn a few pence for their efforts. The Burrell family from Westcott is seen here at work in the field.

Six of the indoors staff at Leylands in Wotton pose in the garden. Seated in the centre is Ellen Rose, wife of Walter, who is the only one not wearing a lace cap, perhaps denoting her seniority. All, of course, wear the familiar starched white aprons of the maid-servant.

Brickworks, Westcott. Weald clay and gault gave rise to many brick-making works, and there are records of a flourishing brickyard situated 1 mile north of Abinger Hall in the early twentieth century. Bricks appear to have been in use in the area since the fifteenth century, many taking the form of brick-noggin – an oak frame filled with brick, sometimes with a coating of plaster. A sales catalogue for The Rookery estate in 1894 gives the following description: 'Lot 11. A valuable enclosure of meadow land. Part of the land on which their (*sic*) stands a kiln has been used as a brick yard, and as there is a good supply of earth, the revival of this manufacture combined with building operations might be profitably carried out.'

Nurses Young, Wilcox and Ward. After much resistance, Dorking Urban District Council constructed a twenty-two-bed isolation hospital in Logmore Lane, Westcott, providing care for patients with infectious diseases such as diphtheria and scarlet fever. It is not clear whether these nurses served at the hospital or were district nurses.

Coming across Sandrock, Westcott, is the carrier Morris Charman, with his wagon hauled by a pair of donkeys. He was employed by The Rookery until an accident on Coast Hill left him with two broken legs, after which he was given the wherewithal to establish his own carting business.

Staff at Hazel Hall, Peaslake. Eight members of staff indicate that this was a medium sized house by Victorian mansion standards.

Balchin & Sons, butchers, 1900. Southdown House on Westcott Green housed the village butcher, seen displaying carcasses outside the premises – enough to give today's environmental health officers a fit of apoplexy. The building remains, although the shop frontage was removed in 1966.

A herdsman proudly shows one of his charges to the camera. The line of the North Downs can be seen in the distance.

Before the sale of the land for building, this fine barn at Bookham was moved to a new site by winching it along on rollers. Upon reaching its destination the structure was jacked up to form the upper storey of a house now named Moorings.

Dorking Laundry staff. The laundry was situated on the Cotmandene at what is now known as Lime Tree Cottage. The spotless aprons bear testimony to the quality of service provided by these hard-working ladies, who never knew the luxury of automatic washing machines.

Jeater's was a family business described as 'glazier, sanitary engineer and house decorator'. It operated from these premises on Main Road, Westcott, now known as Penny Cottage. Founded in 1862, the firm traded here until 1966.

Hoopshaver in Deerleap Woods. The hoopshaver was one of a number of itinerant woodsmen whose livelihood was made possible by a careful use of sustainable woodland. 'Copse cutting is one of the handy labourer's winter harvests, and is done by piecework. One of the industries that grows out of it is hoop making. . . . It is the making of hoops for barrels and cases; hoops shaved on both sides and made up in neat bundles of standard lengths. The shavings make a capital and durable thatch. Hoop making, which is still carried on in the woods of the district on a rather large scale, is probably not an ancient industry. It must have grown with the modern facilities for communication, for the largest and longest hoops go to the tropics for sugar hogsheads.' (Gertrude Jekyll, *Old West Surrey*.)

The shelter for this group of itinerant hoopshavers was made from the debris of their day's work in Deerleap Woods at Wotton.

Walter Rose's brother Ernest was a gardener at Holcombe, a large house in Westcott. He is pictured here splendidly attired in apron and bowler hat in one of the greenhouses at Holcombe.

Reigate Industrial & Provident Society Ltd. Dorking's first co-operative store, opened in 1904, was to be found on the rise behind the area where the bandstand stood in South Street, and formed part of Stapleton House. The upper storey of the store was given over to the YWCA.

The interior of the Reigate Industrial & Provident Society Ltd shop. All the provisions on offer are packaged in wooden, tin, paper or glass containers.

Woodlands, Westcott, 1908. This fine, solid Edwardian house appears to be complete, but work is continuing on the landscaping of the garden.

Vi Taylor, 1904. Her father was employed at Springfield Farm, Westcott, where Vi was pictured with a calf.

Milton Farm, Westcott, 1905. Kent & Chalke's haymaking gang is in the field that was to become the residential Milton Avenue.

Hand reaping, Westcott. Machines were now commonplace in the fields, bringing much easier working conditions for the farm labourer. Gertrude Jekyll recalls: 'One of the few changes in the form and use of hand tools that has occurred within my recollection has been in those used for the reaping of corn. Before my time, but well into the early half of the last century, wheat was reaped with the sickle. It was shaped like the reaping-hook, but had a finely toothed edge. The underside of the blade towards the edge was a saw. When I was a biggish child, strong and delighting in any bodily exercise, I sometimes had a day in the harvest field. Anyone who has never done a day's work in the harvest field would scarcely believe what dirty work it is. Honest sweat and dry dust combine into a mixture not unlike mud. Hay making is drawing-room work in comparison.'

The firm of C. Bassett from Wadhurst in Sussex carries out repairs to the spire of Westcott church, 1914. Ascent was by wooden ladders bound together with ropes, and the summit was crowned by a wooden platform up to which the repair materials were hoisted.

Westcott Volunteer Fire Brigade, 1914. The following article was printed in the *Dorking Advertiser* on 3 December 1912: 'The fire engine which Dorking Urban Council have kindly loaned to the Westcott Volunteer Fire Brigade was formally handed over on Tuesday evening. Manned by Dorking firemen and accompanied by their second engine conveying other members, it arrived in the village at 7.30 and a good number of residents assembled to witness the drills by the combined brigades under Chief Officer Whaley (Dorking), and Chief Officer Brooks (Westcott). Considering their little opportunity of previous practice with an engine, Westcott Brigade acquitted themselves in a very praiseworthy manner, affording every promise now that they are better equipped that they will be able to render, in case of emergency, far more effectual service than has hitherto been the case. The engine, which is to remain in the possession of the Westcott Brigade, was tested by wet drill and found to be in capital condition, considering its forty years' service.'

Charles Collins in his studio. Many of the paintings that Collins exhibited at the Royal Academy and at London exhibitions were painted in his studio at Horsham Road, Dorking. The painting that he appears to be working on shows two of his children at the River Mole, Westhumble, and can be seen in the Dorking and District Museum, West Street, Dorking.

Members of staff from Arthur Brooke's residence, Leylands at Wotton, are pictured on a Sunday visit to the local tourist haunt of Leith Hill Tower.

Leith Hill. 1911

Bonfire on Leith Hill, 1911. Across the land beacons blazed in celebration of the coronation of King George V, and Coldharbour people built this beautifully constructed bonfire next to the Tower.

The year was 1897 and the occasion was Queen Victoria's Diamond Jubilee. Great festivity was about to sweep the nation and villagers built this celebration arch in Westcott Street.

Wotton Cricket Club, 1908. The Evelyns were obviously patrons of the club, for their crest can be seen at the top of the central arch on the charming thatched pavilion. The cricket ground was sited to the side of the main drive leading to Wotton House.

A gathering of ladies pose alongside the Mission Hall in St John's Road, Westcott, 1912. Such well-known local families as Worsfold, Hubbard, Razell, Bridger and Rose are represented here.

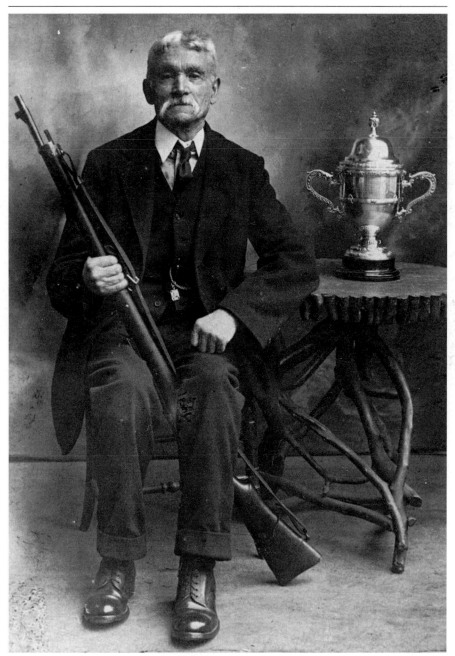

Mr Sawyers worked as a blacksmith on Westcott Common and was a keen member of Westcott Rifle Club. Rumour has it that the club disbanded shortly after a target was found to have 'bullet' holes made in it with a nail, in order to record a higher score during a shooting match.

Wotton Hatch

A hunt meeting at Wotton Hatch was photographed by Walter Rose in around 1900. It was published by Francis Frith & Co., but bore Rose's name – unusual for this large postcard publisher, which rarely carried any other names but its own despite using many different photographers throughout the land. 'The retrograde character of Wotton can be understood when we consider their almost entire dependence on agricultural pursuits. Surrey is not by any means alone in showing a somewhat alarming decrease of population in its more remote rural districts.' (Ellen Smith, *The Reigate Sheet*.) Wotton's population in 1871 was 711, falling to 608 by the year 1901.

Peace celebrations, 1919. With the carnage of the First World War finally at an end, a wave of celebratory euphoria swept across the nation. Farm carts, bicycles and babies' prams were draped in flags and festooned with wild flowers before a procession through the village.

A visit from the travelling showmen was always a thrill, and here they have just set up the rides as the steam-driven gallopers appear to have no customers. The children looking on are no doubt anticipating an evening of fun and laughter.

Johnsons', the provisions supplier on Westcott Green, helped with fund-raising for Dorking Hospital in July 1899. The poster in the shop window announces 'a cricket match on the Cotmandene, with music provided by Dorking Town Band'.

A caravan at Leylands, provided as overnight accommodation for lady cyclists by Arthur Brooke. 'Women were now beginning to ride bicycles and many people were so greatly shocked at it that numbers of country inn-keepers would not give them shelter. A number of girls had formed themselves into the "Mowbray House Cycling Association". . . . Here Arthur felt that we could be really useful; we had a nice caravan fitted up with four beds, a wash stand, a bath in the floor, an oil cooking stove and all necessary crockery etc. It was put in a field close to the garden and a square tent was added for a dining room. Such nice girls used to come up and we greatly enjoyed their visits. This lasted for some years and then the MHCA was given up because there was no more need of it, women were bicycling everywhere and the shocked ones were no longer shocked.' (Alice Brooke, 1929.)

Thomas, Ellen and Robert Wyvill Barclay in the grounds of Bury Hill House, 1898. Rising to the rank of Major during the First World War, Thomas was returning home on leave in 1917 when his ship HM *Transport Transylvania* was sunk by a torpedo in the Mediterranean. Thomas reached a raft, but realizing that it was overloaded with men he had helped rescue he swam behind it, endeavouring to guide it through the rough seas. Help did not arrive for three and a half hours, and Major Thomas died of exhaustion. His Majesty the King posthumously awarded him the Board of Trade Silver Medal for Gallantry in Saving Life at Sea.

Hi-fi, *c.* 1900. So proud was this man of his newly acquired Edison Home Phonograph that he took it to Walter Rose's studio to be photographed. Lighting was provided by daylight coming through roof lights to the right. The table is featured as a prop in many photographs and was made by Walter. A handbill of the day advertised, 'Edison's Phonograph in Dorking – this marvellous instrument made at Edison's factory will be exhibited daily at 7 High Street, Dorking, between the hours of 10 a.m. and 10 p.m. Admission free – but a small charge will be made for each performance.'

Baby show, Dorking. A group of entrants with their proud parents or nannies are outside the Friends' Meeting House, Butter Hill. Formal Sunday dress was the order of the day, although the old bonnets worn by the senior ladies had been replaced by jaunty boaters among the younger folk.

The owners of The Willows in Westcott Street played host to this group of guests at a garden party. How hot they all must have become wearing the fashion of the day – men in heavy three piece suits, collars and ties, while the women favoured long dresses, high necked blouses and large hats.

Walter Rose, in front of the camera for a change, proudly standing among his beehives, 1908. 'By local custom a wandering swarm, worth from eight to ten shillings, is the property of anyone on whose place it settles, though of course it is not claimed among good neighbours when the one who hives it knows where it came from. But often a swarm flies far before settling. Any clanging noise is supposed to stop its flight and induces it to come down, and there was thought to be a special attraction about the noise of an old ploughshare beaten on with a heavy door key.' (Gertrude Jekyll, *Old West Surrey*.)

A tranquil summer scene on the River Mole below Box Hill, as an artist whiles away the day painting from his rowing boat under the shade of a parasol.

Another fine picture of the servants at Arthur Brooke's house, Leylands, at Wotton.

Kempslade Farm, Friday Street. The rarity of a photographer visiting is clearly indicated in this picture, where everyone has stopped for Walter Rose's camera. 'Formerly, within a mile or two of one's home, it was a rare thing to see a stranger, and people's lives went leisurely. Now, the strain and throng and unceasing restlessness that have been induced by all kinds of competition and by ease of communication, have invaded this quiet corner of the land.' (Gertrude Jekyll, *Old West Surrey*.)

The wife of miller Arthur Crane draws water from the stream feeding their mill at Abinger, which was derelict by the early twentieth century. All that remains today at this site is the mill cottage.

Ewhurst Mill. The present tower mill dates from around 1845, after the previous post mill was blown down in a gale. It is said that the miller, who was inside the mill at the time, neglected to turn the sails into the wind, with disastrous results. The mill ceased working around 1885 and was converted into a residence in around 1900.

A fellow photographer with his camera case over his shoulder provided the focal point for this picture, taken on a bridge over the Tillingbourne in Shere village.

The Angel Inn, Woodhatch, is now at a busy crossroads on the A217 south of Reigate, carrying much traffic to Gatwick Airport and the south coast. Pevsner said of this building in 1962: 'On the main road south of the town is The Angel, Woodhatch, a very queer half-timbered building and almost like a folly. Very tall and thin three deep storeys and a gable with two lean-to's giving the effect of a clerestory. Regular timbering, possibly of *c.* 1650. Oddly deliberate and formal especially for south-east England.' The building became an inn in the eighteenth century and bore the sign of The White Horse, changing to its present title around 1814.

Park Farm, Wotton. Situated just below the North Downs, this farm was owned by the Sparks family, a member of which can be seen in this picture. The barn on the right is of some importance and is now a listed building. The Sparks family left the farm following the death of Mr Sparks from shotgun wounds at Pickett's Hole. At the inquest into his death the coroner returned an open verdict.

Disused since 1842, Albury church dates chiefly from the Norman period and the thirteenth century, while the north walls of the nave and base of the tower are believed to be Saxon. The south transept was restored in the nineteenth century with brilliant wall decorations and stained glass. There are some early brasses and seventeenth- and eighteenth-century memorials.

Crossways Farm, Abinger. Built in around 1622 by either the Lee or Atlee family, this house has a particularly noticeable façade, being an outstanding example of contemporary vernacular detail in brick. It has been described as 'possibly one of the most perfect small Jacobean houses in Surrey, which it is said George Meredith used as a background for *Diana of the Crossways*'. The recently restored barn adjacent to the farmhouse dates from much the same time, and contrary to the popular trend continues to be used for agricultural purposes.

One of the many views of Westcott church taken by Walter Rose depicts the vestry (on the right), which dates it to around 1890.

Heath Hill, Dorking, *c.* 1890. These much photographed dwellings in an old corner of Dorking were swept away in the 1960s to make way for flats.

The Surrey Oaks, Parkgate. Formerly a house and wheelwrights (Butcher's), it changed to brewing and opened as a public house in the 1850s. The property was sold to the Horsham brewers King & Barnes in 1912. The pub's name serves as a reminder of the importance of timber to the rural economy. The large-scale destruction of much of the Wealden forest caused great concern in the seventeenth century and led John Evelyn (of Wotton) to write his famous book *Sylva*, which became the standard work on English trees. Ewood, barely a mile north of Parkgate, was one of the principal iron-ore smelting mills in the area, and in 1581 prohibitive measures designed to check the destruction of forests were passed. An exemption was made for the woods of 'Christopher Darrell, gentleman, in the parish of Newdigate within the weald of the countie of Surrie which woods of the said Christopher have heretofore beene, and be by him preserved and coppised for the use of his iron-works in these parts'. Darrell died in 1581 in reduced circumstances, which had led to his becoming indebted to the Crown. It would appear, therefore, that the Queen had a definite interest in the property, which may explain the special exemption in the Act of 1581.

Holmbury St Mary church. Formerly two hamlets, Felday and Pitland Street, the area became known by its present title after George Edmund Street built the church, dedicated to St Mary, in memory of his second wife in 1879. The clock was installed in 1887 to celebrate Queen Victoria's Golden Jubilee.

Shere church recently celebrated its 800th anniversary, but the Domesday Book makes reference to an earlier Saxon church. Built in 1190 in Early English style and dedicated to St James, the church has seen alterations since the thirteenth century. Among the most notable internal features are the fourteenth-century quatrefoil and squint in the north wall, through which it is said that Christine the anchoress made contact with the church from the confines of her cell. Parish registers date back to 1547, and the names of the rectors to 1270.

Walter Rose spent his life in Westcott Street, a short walk from this viewpoint. He took this photograph before the advent of the motor car, which was to turn this tranquil village into one bisected by the major east–west traffic route in the county. Only the construction of the M25 brought some relief to the congestion that ensued. The Surrey Trading Company's offices were demolished in 1975, but the other buildings still remain.

Sleepy Hollow, Abinger. A picturesque spot just south of Crossways Farm, this was much favoured by photographers at the turn of the century, due in some part to a photograph taken in 1887 by Col. Joseph Gale, one of the best known and respected photographers in the last quarter of the nineteenth century. Col. Gale's photograph 'Sleepy Hollow' brought him wide acclaim, and in 1888 he became President of the West Surrey Amateur Photographic Association, a factor that may have encouraged the aspiring Walter Rose to emulate Gale's successful depiction of this rural idyll.

Tillingbourne Falls is a man-made feature in the grounds of a house named Lonesome near Broadmore, and in a sales catalogue of the 1790s it was referred to as The Cascade. A team of volunteers has recently cleared the undergrowth and restored the Falls to their former glory.

Heath Rise, Westcott. This was the home of the Grace family at the time of the photograph, and was demolished in 1966. Mr Charlie Beadle was the tenant in 1952 when the opportunity to purchase the property arose, but he considered the asking price of £120 too high.

Paddington Mill Cottages, Abinger. Now known as Kingsland Cottages, these were farm-workers' dwellings, and a good degree of self-sufficiency is shown. 'Sweet-smelling bushes and herbs, such as rosemary, lavender, southernwood, mint, sage and balm, or at least some of them, were to be found in the older cottagers' garden plots. Perhaps southernwood was the greatest favourite of all. An old man said that when he was young he used to put bergamot (*monarda*) into his hair-grease – "Just did please the girls" he said.' (Gertrude Jekyll, *Old West Surrey*.)

Forge, Sutton Abinger. The Collinsons were blacksmiths in this hamlet until 1913, when Mr Etherington took charge of the business. He was here until the 1920s. The increase in motor vehicle ownership heralded the demise of this trade throughout the country.

Mill House, Westcott Street. This view was taken at the rear of this property, showing the occupiers with their two dogs.

The Glade, Holmbury St Mary, *c.* 1900. This view was taken before the majority of houses were built in this road, which leads off the village green. The farm buildings in the foreground no longer stand.

Hole Hill Crossing, Westcott. The crossing-gate keeper, Mr Hubbard, and some relatives stand alongside their neat cottage on the Reading–Tonbridge line. The cottage was demolished in the 1960s.

Newark Mill was a massive wooden construction next to the River Wey Navigation, first specifically recorded in 1677, milling corn until 1839 after which it milled paper. Joseph Jarman took over as miller in 1895 and the business remained in the family until closure in 1943 when a bomb fell nearby and damaged part of the mill. The building lay empty for many years until a massive fire razed it to the ground in December 1966. Within an hour the structure that had stood for 300 years was reduced to a smouldering ruin.

The Rookery, Westcott. 'In the "leafy month of June" the Rookery will be seen in all its glory, for the little islets on the lake are planted with rhododendrons which are then in full bloom. Time was, and not that many years since, when the stranger might ramble at pleasure over almost every portion of the grounds, but the curiosity of sightseers exceeded their discretion and now if the visitor deviate into any one of the bye-ways, he is liable to be warned off. No one can complain of this restriction, for a limit must be fixed somewhere, and it is but just that the proprietor of an estate should be free to enjoy all the charm of its seclusion. And, indeed, it is impossible to speak in terms too eulogistic of the noble manner in which the landowners round Dorking throw open their grounds to the public, and even endeavour in many ways to facilitate access to them. There is nothing remarkable about the house, which is low and roomy.' (*Illustrated Handbook of Dorking*, 1855.)

The Rookery, Westcott. Formerly known as Chert-gate, this house belonged to the Comber family in the eighteenth century. They sold the property to Abraham Tucker of Betchworth Castle. Daniel Malthus purchased the house and estate in 1759, embellishing it and renaming it The Rookery. Sold in 1768 to Richard Fuller, the property changed hands variously after 1894, during which period it was tenanted by, among others, Lord Wolverton. The *Dorking Advertiser* reported: 'In June 1904, King Edward VII and Queen Alexandra visited by motor-car for tea, and on both the outward and return journeys the royal couple were recognized by only a very few people, for they wore goggles and Her Majesty sported a fawn dust-cloak with hat to match.' The house was demolished in 1966, and an undistinguished row of houses now stands on the site.

Leylands, Wotton. A substantial house, providing 'places' for many local people, it was built in the seventeenth century and latterly owned by Arthur Brooke, whose father founded the Brooke-Bond tea company. The family moved to The Rookery in the first decade of the twentieth century.

Fire at Leylands, Wotton. The *Dorking Advertiser* carried this report on Saturday 9 October 1909: 'Extensive damage estimated at several hundreds of pounds was caused by a fire which occurred at the motor garage at Leylands, Wotton, the residence of Mr A. Brook JP, the garage and stables, together with the coachman's living rooms over, being razed to the ground. Mr Halkett of Shootlands immediately despatched his motor car to Dorking to summon the fire brigade. Captain Rowe and two firemen proceeding at once in the motor car to the scene of the fire, with reels of hose and appliances. The firemen were able to get to work with a delivery just in time to save the nurse's cottage from the same fate which had befallen the adjoining buildings. Within a very few moments of the outbreak, the garage literally became a furnace, and it was impossible to remove a 40 hp Opal motor car. The coachman, William Harley, however, succeeded in rescuing a horse from the adjoining stables. It may be mentioned that among the large numbers of persons attracted to the fire was Mr J.H.C. Evelyn JP, who offered to send his engine and men from Wotton House, but happily this assistance was not required.'

The Common, Westcott. Mrs Ellen Rose and a young friend walk the path up to Westcott church. Behind them is the main (A25) road with Ryde's forge on the left and the Cricketers pub on the right.

The Cricketers, Westcott, *c.* 1880. This must be one of Rose's earliest surviving glass plates, and its patchy appearance indicates that it was probably coated by Walter Rose using the wet-collodion process. Originally faced in warm red brick, the outward appearance of the pub has been changed to its detriment by the current trend to paint all building exteriors cream. The landlady at this time was Martha Coleman.

Westcott midwife, Mrs Ansell, draws water from the well of her Milton Street cottage. Each cottage may have had its own well, and where the water was close to the surface it was reached by lowering a pail by a pole with a spring hook at the end, or if deeper with a winch and rope.

Mr J. Evelyn MP, owner of Wotton House and descendant of the diarist John Evelyn, asked Walter Rose to take a photograph of his recently introduced novelty item – Indian cattle. His payment was a brace of pheasants.

Aylmer's (Elmer's) Mill, Ockley. An octagonal smock mill, built in 1803 for Robert Harrison, this provided ground corn for the large estates of Ockley Court, Jayes Park and Broome Hall. The last miller was Edward Coldman, who ceased trading around 1908 and the mill fabric rapidly deteriorated. Despite attempts to preserve it the mill collapsed suddenly, allegedly in a dead calm, on 23 November 1944.

High Street, Cobham. Hardly any of these buildings still stand, as a result of 'modernization' in the 1960s.

Gomshall Mill, *c.* 1905. Anybody passing by the mill today would certainly have to look twice to recognize it from this photograph – taken before the road bridge was built to cross the Tillingbourne, replacing the simple footbridge shown here. Partly seventeenth-century in construction, this mill originally had two water wheels, one of which was scrapped in 1939. Mr Egerton worked the mill until the late 1940s, after which time it lay derelict until restoration work started in 1964. It is now a popular antiques, gift and tea-shop.

Abe Wright was Westcott's road sweeper in the 1920s, and the litter-free verges are remembered by some with fondness.

Logmore Farm, 1905. Farmed at this period by the Tunnell family, it was subsequently owned by Lord Helsby, a staunch supporter of the Labour Party.

The Dowager Marchioness of Hertford, photographed in the garden of her home, Brooklands, Westcott, with her daughter, Lady Florence Blunt, who was a lady-in-waiting to Queen Victoria. The Dowager Marchioness died in 1901.

Cobham Mill was built in 1822 alongside a large mill of much earlier origin. Milling ceased in 1928 after which time the buildings were used as storage and a shop by Henry Moore & Son, seed merchants, purveyors of animal feed and bedding. The shop was demolished by a Canadian tank in the 1940s when the coal merchants, Hutchinsons, were using the buildings for storage. Surrey County Council compulsorily purchased the whole mill complex in 1953 and demolished the main building to allow the road to be widened, leaving the smaller mill isolated and derelict. In 1973 the Cobham Conservation Group was formed with the intent of preserving the mill, but shortage of funds hampered their activities. By 1986 the Thames Water Authority (now National Rivers Authority) needed to rebuild the weirs at Cobham, so purchased the freehold of the Grade II listed building. They agreed to rescue the fabric of Cobham Mill, while the newly formed Cobham Mill Preservation Trust embarked upon a process of lengthy repair works to the machinery, beginning by raising the rims of the waterwheel in September 1990. The mill was restored to working order and opened to the public in May 1993.

Wintershaw, Westcott, 1900. A Miss Carmichael sold this house with its well-known cherry orchard to a Mrs Pringle in 1910. Three servants posed for Walter Rose's camera.

Broadmoor, 1890. The cottages were built as a philanthropic development in the 1880s by Arthur Brooke around a central reading room. 'Scores of pedestrians now pass through this hamlet in the summer time, as there are radiating from it two pathways leading respectively to Leith Hill and Friday Street. . . . Tourists walking from Dorking or Westcott to Friday Street find Broadmoor a convenient half-way house for rest and refreshment; and though some of the cottages offer shelter from the noon-day heat under the fruit trees in their gardens, there is not yet sufficient accommodation for the ever-increasing number who pass this way.' (Ellen Smith, *The Reigate Sheet*.)

Coming towards the camera carrying a yolk with milk pails hanging either side is Zephaniah Greenstreet, dubbed the 'Sabbatical Milkman' because he rested his donkey on Sundays and delivered milk in the age-old fashion. Zephaniah farmed at Cradhurst and also managed to fill the role of pound-keeper.

Church Street, Dorking. This row of cottages was demolished in the 1930s to make way for a small industrial development, which itself was cleared to allow for sheltered housing in the 1980s.

BURY HILL HOUSE.

Bury Hill House. This splendid mansion, built in 1753, was home to the Barclay family between 1805 and 1952. The central portion was gutted by fire in 1959 but the other sections were untouched and have been converted into apartments. Behind the house on the far right can be seen the observatory built by Decimus Burton in 1846 for Arthur Kett Barclay, a keen astronomer. This building was substantially rebuilt in 1990.

MILTON FARM.

Milton Farm, Westcott. Kent & Chalke were notable as growers of peppermint at Milton Farm until 1907. The crop was harvested by hand, using scythes with finely toothed blades, being fragile and easily bruised. It was then packed into 'Russian mats' similar to hop pockets, ready for transporting to the distillery, usually the one at Mitcham. For a period, though, Milton Farm had its own still.

Leith Hill Tower. Visitors to this eighteenth-century folly were able to buy refreshments from the tea-shop at the foot of the tower, which stood 967 ft above sea level, the stiff climb ensuring the tea-shop a brisk trade. The tower was built in 1765 by the owner of Leith Hill Place, Richard Hull, and his body was interred in the tower upon his death in 1772. Embellishments were carried out by the landowner, W.J. Evelyn, in 1864, allowing glorious views from the turret, 1,031 ft above the Wealden countryside.

Abinger Mill, an ancient three-storey building, was demolished around the time of the First World War. The apex of the roof was situated just above the level of the mill pond, ensuring a good fall of water. 'The water flour-mills are usually buildings of some antiquity, and nearly always of interest in some way or other. Indeed, the mere fact of the placing of the mill, with its pond above and its stream below, and the working of it – the water dashing in the great wheel, the sound of the old-time mill machinery, the constant vibration as of something alive (some sort of plodding, lumbering, good-natured, meal-producing monster, fed and guided and controlled by the careful miller), the pleasant smell, the light dimmed by the floating floury particles – all these sights and sounds and impressions make a water corn-mill a place where the imagination is stimulated to something akin to a poetical apprehension of the ways of the older industries that have gone on almost unchanged for a thousand years.' (Gertrude Jekyll, *Old West Surrey*.)

Kingscote, Westcott Street. This sixteenth-century house was the home of Dr Waterhouse until the 1920s.

Rookery Farm, Westcott, 1910. Westcott Mill pond is in the foreground, the mill having ceased working in 1905 under the ownership of Mr C.B. Hall. A gas driven engine had recently been installed to drive the mill when no head of water was available, but was accidentally engaged when the head was good, resulting in the stripping of the mill gears.

Pictured in the twilight of his life by Dolly, Walter Rose strikes the pose of the artist, poised at his easel, 'working' on an oil painting that he had in fact finished several years earlier.

Acknowledgements

Cobham Mill Preservation Trust, *Cobham Mill*
Dorking Advertiser
Farries, K.G. and Mason, M.T., *The Windmills of Surrey and Inner London*, Charles Skilton Ltd (1966)
Jackson, Alan, *Around Dorking in Old Photographs*, Alan Sutton Publishing, Stroud (1989)
Jekyll, Gertrude, *Old West Surrey*, Kohler and Coombes, Dorking (1904)
Pevsner, N. and Nairn, I., *The Buildings of England: Surrey*, Penguin Books (1962)
Smith, Ellen, *The Reigate Sheet of the one-inch Ordnance Survey*, A. & C. Black, London (1910)
Stidder, Derek, *The Watermills of Surrey*, Barracuda Books (1990)

The photograph captions were compiled in collaboration with David Knight, whose assistance has been invaluable.
   Because most of these photographs have been printed from their original glass-plate negatives, beautiful hand-made prints can be obtained from the author at: Goodness Gracious, Jayes Park Courtyard, Lake Road, Ockley, Surrey, RH5 5RR. Tel. (0306) 621474.